Emma Watson

ABDO
Publishing Company

Big Buddy BOOKS
Buddy Bios

by Sarah Tieck

VISIT US AT
www.abdopublishing.com

Published by ABDO Publishing Company, 8000 West 78th Street, Edina, Minnesota 55439.

Printed in the United States of America, North Mankato, Minnesota.
112009
012010

 PRINTED ON RECYCLED PAPER

Coordinating Series Editor: Rochelle Baltzer
Contributing Editors: Heidi M.D. Elston, Megan M. Gunderson, BreAnn Rumsch, Marcia Zappa
Graphic Design: Maria Hosley
Cover Photograph: *AP Photo*: Joel Ryan
Interior Photographs/Illustrations: *AP Photo*: Tammie Arroyo (p. 24), Jaap Buitenpjik/Warner Bros. (p. 17), Murray Close/Warner Bros. (p. 16), Alastair Grant (pp. 21, 25), Jennifer Graylock (p. 9), Anthony Harver (p. 21), Daria Khazei (p. 13), John D. McHugh (p. 18), Matt Sayles (p. 23), Sipa via AP Images (p. 21), Dan Steinberg (p. 5), Charles Sykes (p. 27), Nick Ut (p. 19), Ian West/PA (p. 29); *Getty Images*: L. Cohen/WireImage (p. 7), Courtesy of Warner Bros./Newsmakers (p. 14), Win Initiative/Photodisc (p. 9); *iStockphoto.com*: ©iStockphoto.com/dsafanda (p. 26), ©iStockphoto.com/Tobiesmom (p. 11); *Shutterstock*: Joy Brown (p. 27).

Library of Congress Cataloging-in-Publication Data

Tieck, Sarah, 1976-
 Emma Watson : Harry Potter star / Sarah Tieck.
   p. cm.
 ISBN 978-1-60453-974-5
 1. Watson, Emma, 1990- Juvenile literature. 2. Actors--Great Britain--Juvenile literature. I. Title.
 PN2598.W25T34 2010
 791.4302'8092--dc22
 [B]
                              2009036370

Emma Watson

Contents

Rising Star

Emma Watson is a talented actress. She has appeared in several movies. She is best known for starring in the Harry Potter movies.

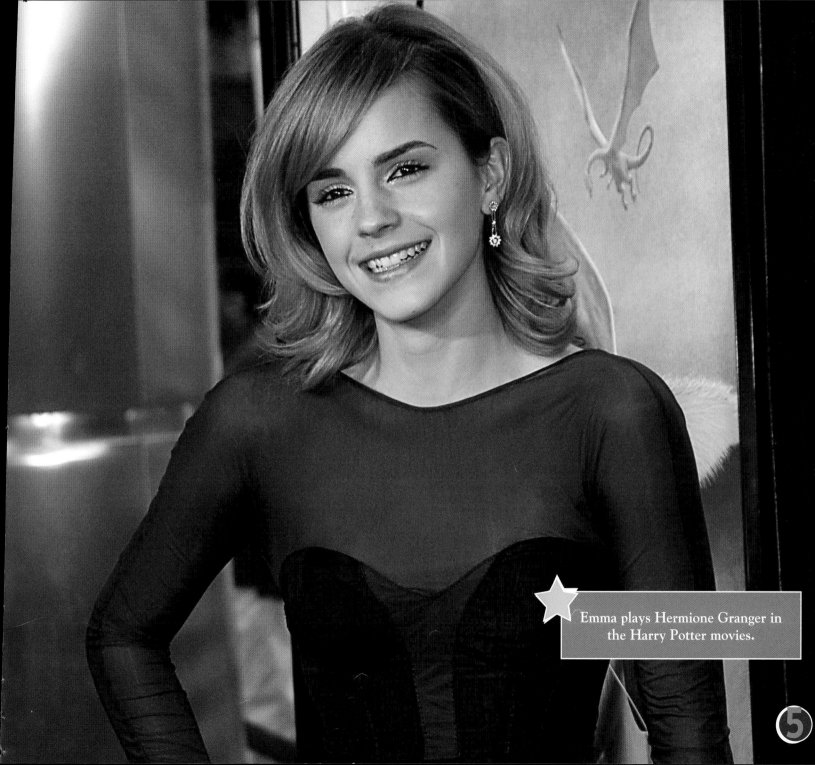

Emma plays Hermione Granger in the Harry Potter movies.

Family Ties

Emma Charlotte Duerre Watson was born in Paris, France, on April 15, 1990. Emma is the daughter of Jacqueline Luesby and Chris Watson. She has a younger brother named Alex.

Emma enjoys spending time with her family.

Growing Up

Emma's family lived in Paris until she was five years old. After her parents divorced, the family moved to England. Emma lived with her mom and brother in Oxford.

Sometimes, Emma's brother Alex attends events with her.

Oxford is a famous, historic city in England.

9

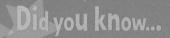
In 1998, Emma started attending Dragon
School in Oxford. She was a good student.
She enjoyed art, **debate**, and field hockey.

At school, people noticed Emma's talent as
a performer. At age seven, she won an award
for performing a poem. She also acted in
school plays.

Field hockey is similar to ice hockey. But instead of ice, it is played on a grassy field. Players use curved sticks to knock a ball into a goal.

Big Break

In 1999, casting agents were hiring actors for the first Harry Potter movie. They visited schools all over England to find child actors.

Emma was asked to **audition** for a **role**. She tried out for the part of Hermione Granger, one of Harry Potter's best friends. Emma auditioned several times before she got the role.

Emma was a fan of the Harry Potter books before she got her role. Her favorite character was Hermione.

Emma was ten when she got the **role** of Hermione. She was very excited! Daniel Radcliffe played Harry Potter. And Rupert Grint played Ron Weasley, Harry's other best friend.

The books and movies follow Harry, Ron, and Hermione as they attend **wizard** school. They share adventures as they battle evil.

Filming soon began for *Harry Potter and the Sorcerer's Stone*. This is the first movie in the Harry Potter **series**.

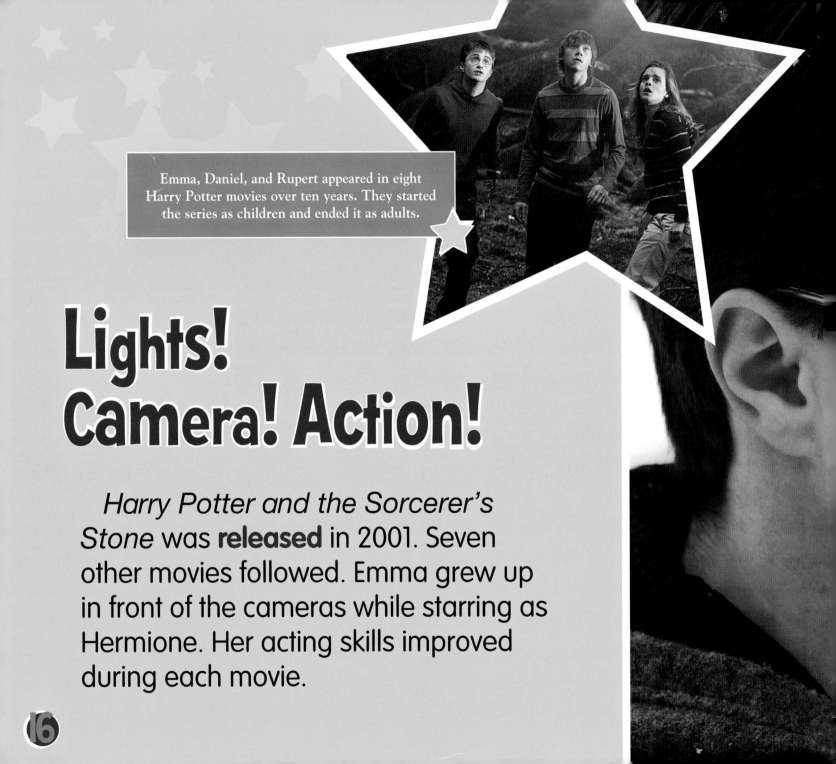

Emma, Daniel, and Rupert appeared in eight Harry Potter movies over ten years. They started the series as children and ended it as adults.

Lights! Camera! Action!

Harry Potter and the Sorcerer's Stone was **released** in 2001. Seven other movies followed. Emma grew up in front of the cameras while starring as Hermione. Her acting skills improved during each movie.

Daniel and Emma became friends while working together on the Harry Potter movies.

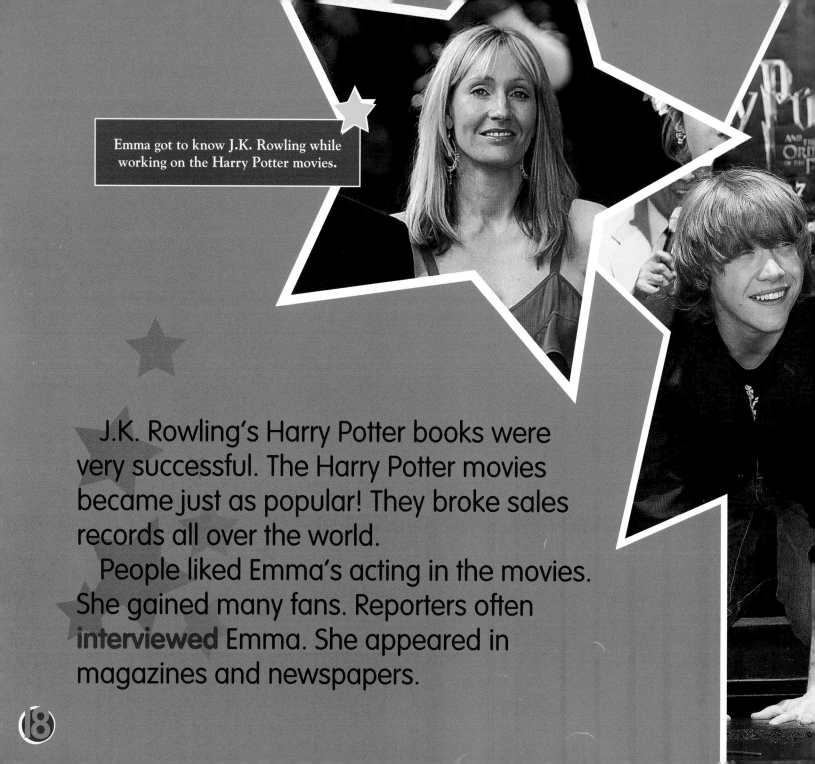

Emma got to know J.K. Rowling while working on the Harry Potter movies.

J.K. Rowling's Harry Potter books were very successful. The Harry Potter movies became just as popular! They broke sales records all over the world.

People liked Emma's acting in the movies. She gained many fans. Reporters often **interviewed** Emma. She appeared in magazines and newspapers.

Rupert, Daniel, and Emma (*left to right*) made prints of their hands and feet in 2007. People can see the prints outside a famous theater in Los Angeles, California.

Fashion Plate

Off the screen, Emma is known for her sense of style. Sometimes actors hire people to help them dress fashionably. But, Emma often enjoys choosing her own outfits.

Emma likes to mix different clothing styles. For example, she combines old-fashioned clothes with trendy items. Her choices are often photographed.

Some of Emma's favorite fashion designs come from Chanel and 3.1 Phillip Lim.

Emma attends fashion shows. Sometimes she even gets to sit in the front row.

An Actress's Life

As an actress, Emma spends time practicing lines and performing. She may be on a movie set several hours each day.

Emma also attends events and meets fans. They often wait in long lines to meet her!

Fans often ask Emma for autographs and pictures.

23

Emma won several awards for her work in the Harry Potter movies. These include a Young Artist Award and a U.K. Nickelodeon Kids' Choice Award.

The Harry Potter movies brought Emma more acting opportunities. In 2007, she had a major **role** in the movie *Ballet Shoes*. Then in 2008, Emma had a voice role in *The Tale of Despereaux*.

The Tale of Despereaux is a cartoon movie. Emma was the voice of Princess Pea.

Harry Potter and the Prisoner of Azkaban won the 2004 Orange Film of the Year award. Emma and producer David Heyman accepted the award.

Scuba divers use special gear so they can breathe and see underwater.

Off the Set

When Emma is not working, she spends time with her family. They have two cats named Bubbles and Domino. Emma enjoys cooking with her dad. She also scuba dives and skis.

Emma likes school, as well. In fall 2009, she took a break from acting to attend college. She left England to begin classes at Brown University in Providence, Rhode Island.

Emma was excited to begin college at Brown University.

Buzz

Emma's fame continues to grow. In July 2009, *Harry Potter and the Half-Blood Prince* was **released**.

That year, Emma filmed *Harry Potter and the Deathly Hallows*. This is the last book in the Harry Potter **series**. It will be released as two movies in 2010 and 2011.

Fans are excited to see what's next for Emma Watson. Many believe she has a bright **future**!

29

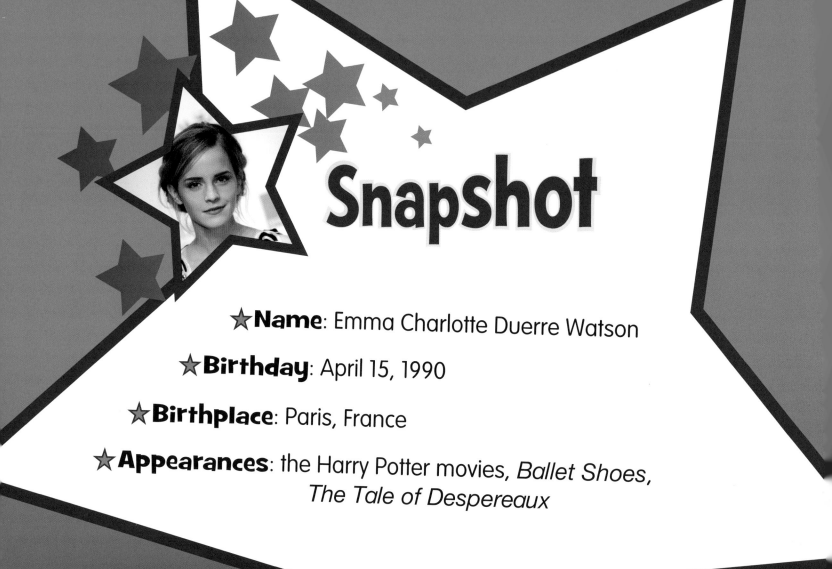

Snapshot

★ **Name**: Emma Charlotte Duerre Watson

★ **Birthday**: April 15, 1990

★ **Birthplace**: Paris, France

★ **Appearances**: the Harry Potter movies, *Ballet Shoes*, *The Tale of Despereaux*

Important Words

audition (aw-DIH-shuhn) to give a trial performance showcasing personal talent as a musician, a singer, a dancer, or an actor.

debate a planned discussion or argument about a question or topic, often held in public.

future (FYOO-chuhr) a time that has not yet occurred.

interview to ask someone a series of questions.

release to make available to the public.

role a part an actor plays.

series a set of similar things or events in order.

set the place where a movie or a television show is recorded.

wizard a person who is skilled in magic.

Web Sites

To learn more about Emma Watson, visit ABDO Publishing Company online. Web sites about Emma Watson are featured on our Book Links page. These links are routinely monitored and updated to provide the most current information available.

www.abdopublishing.com

Index